50 Simple Soups Made from Scratch for the House

By: Kelly Johnson

Table of Contents

- Classic Tomato Soup
- Chicken Noodle Soup
- Potato Leek Soup
- Creamy Broccoli Soup
- Vegetable Minestrone
- French Onion Soup
- Roasted Carrot and Ginger Soup
- Lentil Soup
- Chicken and Rice Soup
- Butternut Squash Soup
- Split Pea Soup
- Corn Chowder
- Cabbage Soup
- Mushroom Soup
- Sweet Potato Soup
- Cream of Spinach Soup
- Clam Chowder
- Beef and Barley Soup
- Roasted Cauliflower Soup
- Egg Drop Soup
- White Bean and Kale Soup
- Zucchini Soup
- Chicken Tortilla Soup
- Tomato Basil Soup
- Sweet Corn and Chicken Soup
- Pumpkin Soup
- Shrimp and Corn Soup
- Pea and Ham Soup
- Thai Coconut Soup
- Beef Stew Soup
- Chicken and Dumpling Soup
- Cream of Celery Soup
- Spinach and Ricotta Soup
- Chicken and Bean Soup
- Spicy Black Bean Soup

- Chicken and Sweet Potato Soup
- Roasted Red Pepper Soup
- Broccoli Cheddar Soup
- Carrot and Parsnip Soup
- Chili Con Carne
- Prawn and Tomato Soup
- Lentil and Tomato Soup
- Tortellini Soup
- Ham and Potato Soup
- Avocado Soup
- Sausage and Kale Soup
- White Chicken Chili
- Eggplant Soup
- Roasted Tomato and Basil Soup
- Sweet Potato and Carrot Soup

Classic Tomato Soup

Ingredients:

- 4 large tomatoes, chopped
- 1 medium onion, chopped
- 3 cloves garlic, minced
- 2 tbsp olive oil
- 4 cups vegetable broth
- 1 tbsp sugar (optional, to balance acidity)
- 1/2 cup heavy cream (optional for creaminess)
- Salt and pepper to taste
- Fresh basil for garnish (optional)

Instructions:

1. In a large pot, heat olive oil over medium heat. Add the onions and garlic, cooking until softened, about 5 minutes.
2. Add the chopped tomatoes and cook for another 5-7 minutes until they begin to break down.
3. Pour in the vegetable broth and bring the mixture to a boil. Lower the heat and simmer for 20-25 minutes.
4. Use an immersion blender to blend the soup until smooth. Alternatively, transfer the soup in batches to a blender and blend.
5. Stir in the sugar, cream, salt, and pepper. Adjust seasoning as needed.
6. Serve warm, garnished with fresh basil if desired.

Chicken Noodle Soup

Ingredients:

- 1 lb chicken breasts or thighs, cooked and shredded
- 1 onion, chopped
- 2 carrots, sliced
- 2 celery stalks, chopped
- 3 cloves garlic, minced
- 6 cups chicken broth
- 1 1/2 cups egg noodles
- 1 tsp dried thyme
- Salt and pepper to taste
- Fresh parsley for garnish (optional)

Instructions:

1. In a large pot, heat a little oil over medium heat. Add onions, carrots, celery, and garlic. Cook until softened, about 5 minutes.
2. Pour in the chicken broth and bring to a boil. Add the shredded chicken, thyme, salt, and pepper. Reduce heat and simmer for 10 minutes.
3. Add the egg noodles and cook according to package instructions, usually about 8-10 minutes.
4. Adjust seasoning with salt and pepper as needed.
5. Serve warm, garnished with fresh parsley if desired.

Potato Leek Soup

Ingredients:

- 4 large potatoes, peeled and diced
- 2 leeks, cleaned and sliced (white and light green parts only)
- 1 medium onion, chopped
- 4 cups vegetable or chicken broth
- 1 cup heavy cream (optional)
- 2 tbsp olive oil
- 2 cloves garlic, minced
- Salt and pepper to taste
- Fresh thyme or parsley for garnish (optional)

Instructions:

1. In a large pot, heat olive oil over medium heat. Add the leeks, onions, and garlic, and cook until softened, about 5 minutes.
2. Add the diced potatoes and broth. Bring to a boil, then reduce the heat and simmer for 20-25 minutes, or until the potatoes are tender.
3. Use an immersion blender to blend the soup until smooth, or carefully transfer to a blender and blend in batches.
4. Stir in heavy cream if desired for a richer texture.
5. Season with salt and pepper to taste.
6. Serve warm, garnished with fresh herbs if desired.

Creamy Broccoli Soup

Ingredients:

- 4 cups broccoli florets
- 1 medium onion, chopped
- 2 cloves garlic, minced
- 4 cups vegetable or chicken broth
- 1 cup milk or cream
- 2 tbsp butter
- Salt and pepper to taste
- Fresh lemon juice (optional)

Instructions:

1. In a large pot, melt butter over medium heat. Add onions and garlic, cooking until softened, about 5 minutes.
2. Add the broccoli florets and broth. Bring to a boil, then reduce heat and simmer for 15-20 minutes, or until the broccoli is tender.
3. Use an immersion blender to blend the soup until smooth, or carefully transfer to a blender and blend in batches.
4. Stir in the milk or cream for a creamy texture.
5. Season with salt, pepper, and a squeeze of lemon juice if desired.
6. Serve warm.

Vegetable Minestrone

Ingredients:

- 2 cups diced carrots
- 1 cup diced celery
- 1 medium onion, chopped
- 1 zucchini, chopped
- 1 can (15 oz) kidney beans, drained and rinsed
- 1 can (15 oz) diced tomatoes
- 4 cups vegetable broth
- 1 cup small pasta (like elbow or ditalini)
- 1 tsp dried oregano
- 1 tsp dried basil
- Salt and pepper to taste
- Fresh parsley for garnish (optional)

Instructions:

1. In a large pot, heat olive oil over medium heat. Add the onions, carrots, celery, and garlic. Cook until softened, about 5 minutes.
2. Add the zucchini, beans, tomatoes, vegetable broth, oregano, and basil. Bring to a boil.
3. Reduce heat and simmer for 15-20 minutes, until the vegetables are tender.
4. Add the pasta and cook according to package instructions.
5. Season with salt and pepper to taste.
6. Serve warm, garnished with fresh parsley if desired.

French Onion Soup

Ingredients:

- 4 large onions, thinly sliced
- 2 tbsp butter
- 1 tbsp olive oil
- 4 cups beef broth
- 1 cup white wine (optional)
- 1 tsp thyme
- Salt and pepper to taste
- 4 slices baguette
- 1 1/2 cups grated Gruyère cheese

Instructions:

1. In a large pot, heat butter and olive oil over medium heat. Add onions and cook, stirring frequently, until caramelized and golden brown, about 25-30 minutes.
2. Add the wine, thyme, salt, and pepper. Cook for another 5 minutes, allowing the wine to reduce slightly.
3. Pour in the beef broth and bring to a boil. Reduce heat and simmer for 10-15 minutes.
4. Preheat your oven's broiler. Place the baguette slices on a baking sheet and toast lightly.
5. Ladle the soup into oven-safe bowls. Top with toasted bread and sprinkle with Gruyère cheese.
6. Place the bowls under the broiler until the cheese is melted and bubbly, about 2-3 minutes.
7. Serve warm.

Roasted Carrot and Ginger Soup

Ingredients:

- 4 large carrots, peeled and chopped
- 1 medium onion, chopped
- 2 tbsp olive oil
- 1-inch piece of fresh ginger, peeled and grated
- 4 cups vegetable broth
- Salt and pepper to taste
- 1/2 tsp ground cumin (optional)

Instructions:

1. Preheat the oven to 400°F (200°C). Toss the carrots with olive oil, salt, and pepper, and roast for 20-25 minutes, or until tender.
2. In a large pot, sauté the onions and ginger in olive oil over medium heat for 5 minutes.
3. Add the roasted carrots and broth. Bring to a boil, then reduce heat and simmer for 10 minutes.
4. Blend the soup until smooth using an immersion blender or in batches in a blender.
5. Season with cumin (optional), salt, and pepper.
6. Serve warm.

Lentil Soup

Ingredients:

- 1 cup dried lentils, rinsed
- 1 onion, chopped
- 2 carrots, diced
- 2 celery stalks, chopped
- 4 cups vegetable or chicken broth
- 1 can (14.5 oz) diced tomatoes
- 1 tsp ground cumin
- Salt and pepper to taste
- Fresh parsley for garnish (optional)

Instructions:

1. In a large pot, sauté the onions, carrots, and celery in olive oil over medium heat for 5 minutes.
2. Add the lentils, broth, diced tomatoes, cumin, salt, and pepper.
3. Bring to a boil, then reduce heat and simmer for 25-30 minutes, or until the lentils are tender.
4. Adjust seasoning with salt and pepper as needed.
5. Serve warm, garnished with fresh parsley if desired.

Chicken and Rice Soup

Ingredients:

- 1 lb chicken breast or thighs, cooked and shredded
- 1 onion, chopped
- 2 carrots, diced
- 2 celery stalks, chopped
- 3 cloves garlic, minced
- 6 cups chicken broth
- 1 cup cooked rice
- Salt and pepper to taste
- Fresh parsley for garnish (optional)

Instructions:

1. In a large pot, sauté the onions, carrots, celery, and garlic in olive oil over medium heat for 5 minutes.
2. Add the chicken broth, cooked chicken, and rice. Bring to a boil, then reduce heat and simmer for 10-15 minutes.
3. Season with salt and pepper to taste.
4. Serve warm, garnished with fresh parsley if desired.

Butternut Squash Soup

Ingredients:

- 1 medium butternut squash, peeled, seeded, and cubed
- 1 onion, chopped
- 2 carrots, sliced
- 2 cloves garlic, minced
- 4 cups vegetable broth
- 1 cup coconut milk (or heavy cream for a richer texture)
- 1 tsp ground cinnamon
- 1/2 tsp ground nutmeg
- Salt and pepper to taste
- Fresh thyme or parsley for garnish (optional)

Instructions:

1. In a large pot, heat olive oil over medium heat. Add the onion, carrots, and garlic, cooking until softened, about 5-7 minutes.
2. Add the butternut squash, vegetable broth, cinnamon, nutmeg, salt, and pepper. Bring to a boil, then reduce the heat and simmer for 20-25 minutes, or until the squash is tender.
3. Use an immersion blender to blend the soup until smooth, or carefully transfer to a blender and blend in batches.
4. Stir in the coconut milk (or cream) for a creamy texture.
5. Adjust seasoning with salt and pepper as needed.
6. Serve warm, garnished with fresh thyme or parsley if desired.

Split Pea Soup

Ingredients:

- 1 1/2 cups dried split peas, rinsed
- 1 onion, chopped
- 2 carrots, diced
- 2 celery stalks, chopped
- 3 cloves garlic, minced
- 1 bay leaf
- 6 cups vegetable or chicken broth
- 1 tsp dried thyme
- Salt and pepper to taste
- 1 ham bone or 1 1/2 cups diced ham (optional)

Instructions:

1. In a large pot, sauté the onion, carrots, celery, and garlic in olive oil over medium heat until softened, about 5 minutes.
2. Add the split peas, broth, bay leaf, thyme, and ham (if using). Bring to a boil, then reduce heat and simmer for 1-1.5 hours, or until the peas are tender and the soup thickens.
3. Remove the ham bone (if using) and discard the bay leaf. If desired, shred the ham from the bone and return it to the soup.
4. Use an immersion blender to blend part of the soup for a creamy texture, or blend in batches.
5. Season with salt and pepper to taste.
6. Serve warm.

Corn Chowder

Ingredients:

- 4 cups corn kernels (fresh or frozen)
- 1 medium onion, chopped
- 2 potatoes, diced
- 2 carrots, chopped
- 2 cloves garlic, minced
- 4 cups vegetable or chicken broth
- 2 cups milk or cream
- 1 tsp thyme
- Salt and pepper to taste
- 2 tbsp butter
- 1/4 cup chopped fresh parsley for garnish (optional)

Instructions:

1. In a large pot, melt butter over medium heat. Add the onion, carrots, and garlic, cooking until softened, about 5 minutes.
2. Add the potatoes, corn, broth, thyme, salt, and pepper. Bring to a boil, then reduce the heat and simmer for 15-20 minutes, or until the potatoes are tender.
3. Stir in the milk or cream and simmer for an additional 5-10 minutes.
4. Use an immersion blender to blend part of the soup for a creamier texture, or blend in batches.
5. Adjust seasoning with salt and pepper as needed.
6. Serve warm, garnished with fresh parsley if desired.

Cabbage Soup

Ingredients:

- 1 small head of cabbage, chopped
- 1 onion, chopped
- 2 carrots, diced
- 2 cloves garlic, minced
- 1 can (14.5 oz) diced tomatoes
- 4 cups vegetable broth
- 1 tsp dried thyme
- 1 tsp paprika
- Salt and pepper to taste
- 1 tbsp olive oil

Instructions:

1. In a large pot, heat olive oil over medium heat. Add the onions, carrots, and garlic, cooking until softened, about 5 minutes.
2. Add the chopped cabbage, tomatoes, vegetable broth, thyme, paprika, salt, and pepper. Bring to a boil, then reduce heat and simmer for 30-40 minutes, or until the cabbage is tender.
3. Adjust seasoning with salt and pepper as needed.
4. Serve warm.

Mushroom Soup

Ingredients:

- 1 lb mushrooms (button or cremini), sliced
- 1 medium onion, chopped
- 2 cloves garlic, minced
- 4 cups vegetable or chicken broth
- 1 cup heavy cream
- 2 tbsp butter
- 1 tbsp fresh thyme or 1 tsp dried thyme
- Salt and pepper to taste

Instructions:

1. In a large pot, melt butter over medium heat. Add the onions and garlic, cooking until softened, about 5 minutes.
2. Add the sliced mushrooms and thyme, cooking for another 8-10 minutes until the mushrooms are tender and browned.
3. Add the broth and bring to a boil. Reduce the heat and simmer for 10 minutes.
4. Stir in the heavy cream and cook for an additional 5 minutes.
5. Use an immersion blender to blend the soup until smooth, or blend in batches for a chunkier texture.
6. Season with salt and pepper to taste.
7. Serve warm.

Sweet Potato Soup

Ingredients:

- 2 large sweet potatoes, peeled and cubed
- 1 onion, chopped
- 2 cloves garlic, minced
- 4 cups vegetable broth
- 1/2 tsp ground cinnamon
- 1/2 tsp ground cumin
- Salt and pepper to taste
- 1 cup coconut milk (optional for a creamy texture)
- Fresh cilantro or parsley for garnish (optional)

Instructions:

1. In a large pot, sauté the onions and garlic in olive oil over medium heat until softened, about 5 minutes.
2. Add the cubed sweet potatoes, vegetable broth, cinnamon, cumin, salt, and pepper. Bring to a boil, then reduce heat and simmer for 20-25 minutes, or until the sweet potatoes are tender.
3. Use an immersion blender to blend the soup until smooth, or carefully transfer to a blender and blend in batches.
4. Stir in the coconut milk (if using) for extra creaminess.
5. Adjust seasoning with salt and pepper as needed.
6. Serve warm, garnished with fresh cilantro or parsley if desired.

Cream of Spinach Soup

Ingredients:

- 4 cups fresh spinach, washed and chopped
- 1 onion, chopped
- 2 cloves garlic, minced
- 4 cups vegetable broth
- 1/2 cup heavy cream
- 1 tbsp butter
- Salt and pepper to taste
- Fresh nutmeg (optional)

Instructions:

1. In a large pot, melt butter over medium heat. Add the onion and garlic, cooking until softened, about 5 minutes.
2. Add the spinach and cook until wilted, about 2-3 minutes.
3. Pour in the vegetable broth and bring to a boil. Reduce heat and simmer for 10 minutes.
4. Use an immersion blender to blend the soup until smooth, or carefully transfer to a blender and blend in batches.
5. Stir in the heavy cream and a pinch of nutmeg (if using).
6. Season with salt and pepper to taste.
7. Serve warm.

Clam Chowder

Ingredients:

- 2 cans (6.5 oz each) clam meat, drained, with juices reserved
- 4 cups clam juice or vegetable broth
- 2 medium potatoes, peeled and diced
- 1 onion, chopped
- 2 celery stalks, chopped
- 2 cloves garlic, minced
- 1 1/2 cups heavy cream
- 4 strips bacon, chopped (optional)
- 1 tbsp butter
- Salt and pepper to taste
- Fresh parsley for garnish (optional)

Instructions:

1. In a large pot, cook the bacon (if using) over medium heat until crispy. Remove and set aside, leaving the bacon drippings in the pot.
2. Add the butter, onions, celery, and garlic to the pot. Cook until softened, about 5 minutes.
3. Add the potatoes, clam juice, and reserved clam juices. Bring to a boil, then reduce heat and simmer for 15-20 minutes, or until the potatoes are tender.
4. Stir in the clams and heavy cream, and cook for an additional 5-7 minutes.
5. Season with salt and pepper to taste.
6. Serve warm, garnished with crispy bacon and fresh parsley if desired.

Beef and Barley Soup

Ingredients:

- 1 lb beef stew meat, cubed
- 1 onion, chopped
- 2 carrots, diced
- 2 celery stalks, chopped
- 3 cloves garlic, minced
- 4 cups beef broth
- 1 cup pearl barley
- 1 can (14.5 oz) diced tomatoes
- 1 tsp dried thyme
- Salt and pepper to taste
- 2 tbsp olive oil

Instructions:

1. In a large pot, heat olive oil over medium heat. Add the beef stew meat and brown on all sides.
2. Add the onions, carrots, celery, and garlic, cooking for about 5 minutes until softened.
3. Pour in the beef broth, barley, tomatoes, thyme, salt, and pepper. Bring to a boil.
4. Reduce heat and simmer for 1-1.5 hours, or until the beef and barley are tender.
5. Adjust seasoning with salt and pepper as needed.
6. Serve warm.

Roasted Cauliflower Soup

Ingredients:

- 1 large head cauliflower, chopped into florets
- 1 medium onion, chopped
- 2 cloves garlic, minced
- 4 cups vegetable or chicken broth
- 1 cup heavy cream or coconut milk
- 2 tbsp olive oil
- Salt and pepper to taste
- Fresh thyme or parsley for garnish (optional)

Instructions:

1. Preheat your oven to 400°F (200°C). Spread the cauliflower florets on a baking sheet and drizzle with 1 tbsp olive oil. Season with salt and pepper, then roast for 25-30 minutes, or until the cauliflower is golden and tender.
2. In a large pot, heat the remaining olive oil over medium heat. Add the onion and garlic, cooking until softened, about 5 minutes.
3. Add the roasted cauliflower to the pot along with the broth. Bring to a boil, then reduce the heat and simmer for 10 minutes.
4. Use an immersion blender to blend the soup until smooth, or transfer in batches to a blender.
5. Stir in the heavy cream or coconut milk, adjusting the seasoning with salt and pepper.
6. Serve warm, garnished with fresh thyme or parsley if desired.

Egg Drop Soup

Ingredients:

- 4 cups chicken broth
- 2 eggs, beaten
- 1 tsp soy sauce
- 1/2 tsp sesame oil
- 1/2 tsp ginger, minced
- 1 green onion, chopped (for garnish)
- Salt and pepper to taste

Instructions:

1. In a large pot, bring the chicken broth to a boil over medium heat. Add the soy sauce, sesame oil, and ginger.
2. Slowly drizzle the beaten eggs into the boiling broth while stirring gently with a fork or chopsticks. The eggs will cook instantly and form silky ribbons.
3. Season with salt and pepper to taste.
4. Serve the soup in bowls, garnished with chopped green onions.

White Bean and Kale Soup

Ingredients:

- 1 can (15 oz) white beans (such as cannellini or great northern), drained and rinsed
- 1 bunch kale, stems removed and leaves chopped
- 1 onion, chopped
- 2 cloves garlic, minced
- 4 cups vegetable or chicken broth
- 1/2 tsp dried thyme
- 1/2 tsp dried rosemary
- 1/2 tsp red pepper flakes (optional)
- 2 tbsp olive oil
- Salt and pepper to taste
- Juice of 1 lemon (optional)

Instructions:

1. Heat olive oil in a large pot over medium heat. Add the onion and garlic, cooking until softened, about 5 minutes.
2. Add the broth, beans, thyme, rosemary, and red pepper flakes. Bring to a boil, then reduce heat and simmer for 10 minutes.
3. Add the chopped kale and cook for an additional 10-15 minutes, or until the kale is tender.
4. Season with salt and pepper to taste. For added brightness, stir in the lemon juice.
5. Serve warm.

Zucchini Soup

Ingredients:

- 3 medium zucchinis, chopped
- 1 onion, chopped
- 2 cloves garlic, minced
- 4 cups vegetable broth
- 1/2 cup heavy cream or coconut milk
- 1 tbsp olive oil
- Salt and pepper to taste
- Fresh basil or parsley for garnish (optional)

Instructions:

1. Heat olive oil in a large pot over medium heat. Add the onion and garlic, cooking until softened, about 5 minutes.
2. Add the chopped zucchini and cook for an additional 5 minutes.
3. Add the vegetable broth and bring to a boil. Reduce heat and simmer for 15-20 minutes, or until the zucchini is tender.
4. Use an immersion blender to blend the soup until smooth, or transfer in batches to a blender.
5. Stir in the cream or coconut milk for a creamy texture.
6. Adjust seasoning with salt and pepper to taste.
7. Serve warm, garnished with fresh basil or parsley if desired.

Chicken Tortilla Soup

Ingredients:

- 2 cups cooked, shredded chicken (rotisserie chicken works well)
- 1 can (14.5 oz) diced tomatoes
- 4 cups chicken broth
- 1 onion, chopped
- 2 cloves garlic, minced
- 1 jalapeño, seeded and chopped (optional)
- 1 tsp ground cumin
- 1/2 tsp chili powder
- 1 tbsp olive oil
- 1/2 cup corn kernels (fresh or frozen)
- Salt and pepper to taste
- Tortilla chips, shredded cheese, sour cream, and cilantro for garnish

Instructions:

1. Heat olive oil in a large pot over medium heat. Add the onion, garlic, and jalapeño (if using), cooking until softened, about 5 minutes.
2. Add the diced tomatoes, chicken broth, cumin, chili powder, corn, and shredded chicken. Bring to a boil, then reduce the heat and simmer for 15 minutes.
3. Season with salt and pepper to taste.
4. Serve the soup in bowls, topped with tortilla chips, shredded cheese, sour cream, and fresh cilantro.

Tomato Basil Soup

Ingredients:

- 4 cups canned tomatoes (or fresh tomatoes, peeled and chopped)
- 1 onion, chopped
- 2 cloves garlic, minced
- 4 cups vegetable or chicken broth
- 1 tsp dried basil (or 1/4 cup fresh basil, chopped)
- 1/2 tsp sugar (optional, to reduce acidity)
- 1/2 cup heavy cream
- 2 tbsp olive oil
- Salt and pepper to taste
- Fresh basil leaves for garnish (optional)

Instructions:

1. In a large pot, heat olive oil over medium heat. Add the onion and garlic, cooking until softened, about 5 minutes.
2. Add the tomatoes, broth, dried basil, and sugar (if using). Bring to a boil, then reduce the heat and simmer for 20 minutes.
3. Use an immersion blender to blend the soup until smooth, or transfer in batches to a blender.
4. Stir in the heavy cream for a creamy texture and adjust seasoning with salt and pepper.
5. Serve warm, garnished with fresh basil leaves if desired.

Sweet Corn and Chicken Soup

Ingredients:

- 2 cups cooked, shredded chicken
- 2 cups corn kernels (fresh, frozen, or canned)
- 4 cups chicken broth
- 1 medium onion, chopped
- 2 cloves garlic, minced
- 1/2 cup heavy cream
- 1 tsp ground cumin
- 1/2 tsp chili powder
- Salt and pepper to taste
- Fresh cilantro for garnish (optional)

Instructions:

1. In a large pot, sauté the onion and garlic in olive oil over medium heat until softened, about 5 minutes.
2. Add the chicken, corn, chicken broth, cumin, and chili powder. Bring to a boil, then reduce heat and simmer for 10-15 minutes.
3. Stir in the heavy cream and cook for an additional 5 minutes.
4. Season with salt and pepper to taste.
5. Serve warm, garnished with fresh cilantro if desired.

Pumpkin Soup

Ingredients:

- 1 can (15 oz) pure pumpkin puree (or 2 cups fresh pumpkin puree)
- 1 onion, chopped
- 2 cloves garlic, minced
- 4 cups vegetable or chicken broth
- 1/2 tsp ground cinnamon
- 1/2 tsp ground nutmeg
- 1/2 cup heavy cream
- 2 tbsp olive oil
- Salt and pepper to taste
- Pumpkin seeds for garnish (optional)

Instructions:

1. In a large pot, heat olive oil over medium heat. Add the onion and garlic, cooking until softened, about 5 minutes.
2. Add the pumpkin puree, broth, cinnamon, and nutmeg. Stir to combine and bring to a boil.
3. Reduce the heat and simmer for 15-20 minutes.
4. Use an immersion blender to blend the soup until smooth, or carefully transfer to a blender.
5. Stir in the heavy cream for a creamy texture.
6. Adjust seasoning with salt and pepper to taste.
7. Serve warm, garnished with pumpkin seeds if desired.

Shrimp and Corn Soup

Ingredients:

- 1 lb shrimp, peeled and deveined
- 1 can (15 oz) corn kernels, drained (or 1.5 cups fresh/frozen corn)
- 4 cups chicken broth
- 1 medium onion, chopped
- 2 cloves garlic, minced
- 1 cup heavy cream
- 1 tsp smoked paprika
- 1/2 tsp chili flakes (optional)
- 1 tbsp olive oil
- Salt and pepper to taste
- Fresh cilantro or parsley for garnish

Instructions:

1. In a large pot, heat olive oil over medium heat. Add the onion and garlic, cooking until softened, about 5 minutes.
2. Add the chicken broth, corn, smoked paprika, and chili flakes. Bring to a boil, then reduce heat and simmer for 10 minutes.
3. Stir in the shrimp and cook for 3-4 minutes, or until the shrimp are pink and cooked through.
4. Add the heavy cream and stir to combine. Season with salt and pepper to taste.
5. Serve warm, garnished with fresh cilantro or parsley.

Pea and Ham Soup

Ingredients:

- 2 cups frozen peas
- 1 cup diced ham
- 4 cups chicken or vegetable broth
- 1 onion, chopped
- 2 cloves garlic, minced
- 2 medium carrots, chopped
- 1 celery stalk, chopped
- 1 tsp dried thyme
- 1 bay leaf
- 1 tbsp olive oil
- Salt and pepper to taste

Instructions:

1. Heat olive oil in a large pot over medium heat. Add the onion, garlic, carrots, and celery, cooking until softened, about 5 minutes.
2. Add the ham, peas, broth, thyme, and bay leaf. Bring to a boil, then reduce heat and simmer for 20-25 minutes.
3. Remove the bay leaf and use an immersion blender to blend the soup until smooth, or transfer in batches to a blender.
4. Season with salt and pepper to taste. Serve warm.

Thai Coconut Soup (Tom Kha Gai)

Ingredients:

- 2 cups chicken breast, sliced thinly
- 4 cups coconut milk
- 2 cups chicken broth
- 1 stalk lemongrass, smashed
- 3-4 kaffir lime leaves (or zest of 1 lime)
- 3-4 slices fresh ginger
- 2-3 Thai bird's eye chilies (optional)
- 1 cup mushrooms, sliced
- 2 tbsp fish sauce
- 1 tbsp brown sugar
- 1 tbsp lime juice
- Fresh cilantro for garnish
- Thai chili slices for garnish (optional)

Instructions:

1. In a large pot, combine the coconut milk, chicken broth, lemongrass, kaffir lime leaves, ginger, and chilies (if using). Bring to a simmer over medium heat.
2. Add the chicken and cook for 5-7 minutes, or until the chicken is cooked through.
3. Stir in the mushrooms, fish sauce, brown sugar, and lime juice. Let it simmer for another 5 minutes.
4. Remove from heat, and remove the lemongrass, ginger, and lime leaves.
5. Garnish with fresh cilantro and chili slices if desired. Serve warm.

Beef Stew Soup

Ingredients:

- 1 lb beef stew meat, cubed
- 4 cups beef broth
- 3 medium potatoes, cubed
- 2 carrots, sliced
- 2 celery stalks, chopped
- 1 onion, chopped
- 2 cloves garlic, minced
- 1 tsp dried thyme
- 1/2 tsp dried rosemary
- 1 bay leaf
- 1 tbsp olive oil
- 1 tbsp tomato paste
- Salt and pepper to taste

Instructions:

1. Heat olive oil in a large pot over medium heat. Brown the beef stew meat in batches, then remove and set aside.
2. In the same pot, add the onion and garlic, cooking until softened, about 5 minutes.
3. Add the tomato paste and cook for 2 minutes, then stir in the beef broth, beef, potatoes, carrots, celery, thyme, rosemary, and bay leaf.
4. Bring to a boil, then reduce heat and simmer for 1.5-2 hours, or until the beef is tender.
5. Season with salt and pepper to taste. Serve warm.

Chicken and Dumpling Soup

Ingredients:

- 2 cups cooked, shredded chicken
- 4 cups chicken broth
- 2 cups whole milk
- 1 onion, chopped
- 2 cloves garlic, minced
- 2 medium carrots, sliced
- 2 celery stalks, chopped
- 1 tsp dried thyme
- 1/2 tsp paprika
- 2 cups all-purpose flour
- 2 tsp baking powder
- 1/2 tsp salt
- 2/3 cup milk
- 2 tbsp butter
- Fresh parsley for garnish

Instructions:

1. In a large pot, sauté the onion and garlic in olive oil over medium heat until softened, about 5 minutes.
2. Add the chicken broth, milk, carrots, celery, thyme, and paprika. Bring to a boil and simmer for 15-20 minutes.
3. In a separate bowl, combine the flour, baking powder, salt, milk, and butter to make the dumpling dough.
4. Drop spoonfuls of the dough into the soup, covering the surface. Reduce heat to a simmer and cook for 10-12 minutes, or until the dumplings are cooked through.
5. Stir in the shredded chicken and cook for another 5 minutes. Season with salt and pepper to taste.
6. Serve warm, garnished with fresh parsley.

Cream of Celery Soup

Ingredients:

- 4 cups celery, chopped
- 1 medium onion, chopped
- 2 cloves garlic, minced
- 4 cups vegetable or chicken broth
- 1 cup heavy cream
- 2 tbsp butter
- 1 tbsp olive oil
- Salt and pepper to taste

Instructions:

1. In a large pot, heat olive oil and butter over medium heat. Add the onion, garlic, and celery, cooking until softened, about 8 minutes.
2. Add the broth and bring to a boil. Reduce the heat and simmer for 15-20 minutes, or until the celery is tender.
3. Use an immersion blender to blend the soup until smooth, or transfer in batches to a blender.
4. Stir in the heavy cream and cook for another 5 minutes.
5. Season with salt and pepper to taste. Serve warm.

Spinach and Ricotta Soup

Ingredients:

- 4 cups fresh spinach
- 1 cup ricotta cheese
- 4 cups vegetable broth
- 1 onion, chopped
- 2 cloves garlic, minced
- 1 tbsp olive oil
- 1/2 tsp nutmeg
- Salt and pepper to taste

Instructions:

1. Heat olive oil in a large pot over medium heat. Add the onion and garlic, cooking until softened, about 5 minutes.
2. Add the vegetable broth and bring to a boil. Reduce the heat and simmer for 10 minutes.
3. Stir in the spinach and cook until wilted, about 5 minutes.
4. Use an immersion blender to blend the soup until smooth, or transfer in batches to a blender.
5. Stir in the ricotta cheese and nutmeg. Cook for an additional 5 minutes, then season with salt and pepper.
6. Serve warm.

Chicken and Bean Soup

Ingredients:

- 2 cups cooked, shredded chicken
- 1 can (15 oz) white beans (such as cannellini or great northern), drained and rinsed
- 4 cups chicken broth
- 1 onion, chopped
- 2 cloves garlic, minced
- 1 tsp cumin
- 1/2 tsp chili powder
- 1/2 tsp paprika
- 1 tbsp olive oil
- Salt and pepper to taste

Instructions:

1. Heat olive oil in a large pot over medium heat. Add the onion and garlic, cooking until softened, about 5 minutes.
2. Add the chicken broth, shredded chicken, beans, cumin, chili powder, and paprika. Bring to a boil, then reduce heat and simmer for 20 minutes.
3. Season with salt and pepper to taste. Serve warm.

Spicy Black Bean Soup

Ingredients:

- 2 cans (15 oz each) black beans, drained and rinsed
- 4 cups vegetable or chicken broth
- 1 onion, chopped
- 2 cloves garlic, minced
- 1 red bell pepper, chopped
- 1 can (10 oz) diced tomatoes with green chilies
- 1 tsp cumin
- 1/2 tsp smoked paprika
- 1/4 tsp cayenne pepper (adjust to taste)
- 1 tbsp olive oil
- Salt and pepper to taste
- Fresh cilantro for garnish
- Lime wedges for serving

Instructions:

1. Heat olive oil in a large pot over medium heat. Add the onion, garlic, and red bell pepper, cooking until softened, about 5 minutes.
2. Stir in the cumin, paprika, and cayenne pepper, cooking for 1-2 minutes until fragrant.
3. Add the black beans, diced tomatoes with green chilies, and broth. Bring to a boil, then reduce heat and simmer for 20 minutes.
4. Use an immersion blender to blend the soup to your desired consistency (smooth or chunky). Alternatively, blend in batches.
5. Season with salt and pepper to taste.
6. Serve warm, garnished with fresh cilantro and lime wedges.

Chicken and Sweet Potato Soup

Ingredients:

- 2 cups cooked, shredded chicken
- 2 medium sweet potatoes, peeled and cubed
- 4 cups chicken broth
- 1 onion, chopped
- 2 cloves garlic, minced
- 1 tsp ground ginger
- 1/2 tsp ground cinnamon
- 1/2 tsp cumin
- 1 tbsp olive oil
- Salt and pepper to taste
- Fresh parsley for garnish

Instructions:

1. Heat olive oil in a large pot over medium heat. Add the onion and garlic, cooking until softened, about 5 minutes.
2. Stir in the ginger, cinnamon, and cumin, and cook for another minute.
3. Add the sweet potatoes and chicken broth. Bring to a boil, then reduce heat and simmer for 20-25 minutes, or until the sweet potatoes are tender.
4. Stir in the shredded chicken and cook for an additional 5 minutes.
5. Use an immersion blender to blend the soup to a smooth consistency or blend in batches.
6. Season with salt and pepper to taste. Serve warm, garnished with fresh parsley.

Roasted Red Pepper Soup

Ingredients:

- 4 red bell peppers, roasted and peeled
- 1 onion, chopped
- 2 cloves garlic, minced
- 4 cups vegetable broth
- 1/2 cup heavy cream (optional for creaminess)
- 1 tbsp olive oil
- 1 tsp smoked paprika
- Salt and pepper to taste
- Fresh basil for garnish

Instructions:

1. Roast the red peppers under a broiler or on a grill until the skins are charred. Let them cool, then peel and remove seeds.
2. Heat olive oil in a large pot over medium heat. Add the onion and garlic, cooking until softened, about 5 minutes.
3. Stir in the smoked paprika and cook for 1 minute.
4. Add the roasted peppers and vegetable broth. Bring to a boil, then reduce heat and simmer for 15 minutes.
5. Use an immersion blender to blend the soup until smooth or blend in batches in a blender.
6. Stir in the heavy cream (if using) and season with salt and pepper to taste.
7. Serve warm, garnished with fresh basil.

Broccoli Cheddar Soup

Ingredients:

- 4 cups broccoli florets
- 4 cups chicken or vegetable broth
- 1 cup grated sharp cheddar cheese
- 1 medium onion, chopped
- 2 cloves garlic, minced
- 1 cup whole milk
- 2 tbsp butter
- 2 tbsp all-purpose flour
- Salt and pepper to taste

Instructions:

1. In a large pot, melt butter over medium heat. Add the onion and garlic, cooking until softened, about 5 minutes.
2. Stir in the flour and cook for 1-2 minutes to make a roux.
3. Gradually add the broth while stirring, bringing to a simmer.
4. Add the broccoli florets and cook for 10-12 minutes, or until tender.
5. Use an immersion blender to blend the soup until smooth or leave it slightly chunky.
6. Stir in the milk and grated cheddar cheese. Continue to cook, stirring until the cheese is melted and the soup is smooth.
7. Season with salt and pepper to taste. Serve warm.

Carrot and Parsnip Soup

Ingredients:

- 4 large carrots, peeled and chopped
- 2 medium parsnips, peeled and chopped
- 4 cups vegetable broth
- 1 onion, chopped
- 2 cloves garlic, minced
- 1 tsp ground cumin
- 1/2 tsp ground coriander
- 1 tbsp olive oil
- Salt and pepper to taste
- Fresh parsley for garnish

Instructions:

1. Heat olive oil in a large pot over medium heat. Add the onion and garlic, cooking until softened, about 5 minutes.
2. Stir in the cumin and coriander, cooking for 1 minute.
3. Add the carrots, parsnips, and vegetable broth. Bring to a boil, then reduce heat and simmer for 25-30 minutes, or until the vegetables are tender.
4. Use an immersion blender to blend the soup until smooth, or blend in batches.
5. Season with salt and pepper to taste. Serve warm, garnished with fresh parsley.

Chili Con Carne

Ingredients:

- 1 lb ground beef or turkey
- 1 onion, chopped
- 2 cloves garlic, minced
- 1 can (15 oz) kidney beans, drained and rinsed
- 1 can (15 oz) black beans, drained and rinsed
- 1 can (15 oz) diced tomatoes
- 2 tbsp chili powder
- 1 tsp cumin
- 1/2 tsp smoked paprika
- 1/2 tsp cayenne pepper (optional)
- 2 cups beef or vegetable broth
- 1 tbsp olive oil
- Salt and pepper to taste
- Sour cream and shredded cheese for garnish (optional)

Instructions:

1. Heat olive oil in a large pot over medium heat. Add the onion and garlic, cooking until softened, about 5 minutes.
2. Add the ground beef or turkey, breaking it up as it cooks until browned.
3. Stir in the chili powder, cumin, paprika, and cayenne (if using). Cook for 1-2 minutes.
4. Add the beans, diced tomatoes, broth, and season with salt and pepper. Bring to a boil, then reduce heat and simmer for 30-40 minutes, stirring occasionally.
5. Serve warm, garnished with sour cream and shredded cheese, if desired.

Prawn and Tomato Soup

Ingredients:

- 1 lb prawns, peeled and deveined
- 4 cups tomato broth or vegetable broth
- 2 cups diced tomatoes (fresh or canned)
- 1 onion, chopped
- 2 cloves garlic, minced
- 1 tsp smoked paprika
- 1/2 tsp dried oregano
- 1 tbsp olive oil
- Salt and pepper to taste
- Fresh parsley for garnish

Instructions:

1. Heat olive oil in a large pot over medium heat. Add the onion and garlic, cooking until softened, about 5 minutes.
2. Stir in the smoked paprika and oregano, cooking for 1 minute.
3. Add the diced tomatoes and broth. Bring to a boil, then reduce heat and simmer for 15 minutes.
4. Add the prawns and cook for an additional 3-5 minutes, or until they are pink and cooked through.
5. Season with salt and pepper to taste. Serve warm, garnished with fresh parsley.

Lentil and Tomato Soup

Ingredients:

- 1 cup dried lentils, rinsed
- 4 cups vegetable broth
- 2 cans (15 oz each) diced tomatoes
- 1 onion, chopped
- 2 cloves garlic, minced
- 2 carrots, chopped
- 2 celery stalks, chopped
- 1 tsp dried thyme
- 1 tsp cumin
- 1 bay leaf
- 1 tbsp olive oil
- Salt and pepper to taste

Instructions:

1. Heat olive oil in a large pot over medium heat. Add the onion, garlic, carrots, and celery, cooking until softened, about 5 minutes.
2. Stir in the thyme, cumin, and bay leaf, cooking for 1 minute.
3. Add the lentils, diced tomatoes, and broth. Bring to a boil, then reduce heat and simmer for 40-45 minutes, or until the lentils are tender.
4. Remove the bay leaf and season with salt and pepper to taste. Serve warm.

Tortellini Soup

Ingredients:

- 1 package (9 oz) cheese tortellini
- 4 cups chicken broth
- 2 cups spinach, chopped
- 1 can (15 oz) diced tomatoes
- 1 onion, chopped
- 2 cloves garlic, minced
- 1 tbsp olive oil
- 1 tsp dried basil
- Salt and pepper to taste
- Grated Parmesan cheese for garnish

Instructions:

1. Heat olive oil in a large pot over medium heat. Add the onion and garlic, cooking until softened, about 5 minutes.
2. Stir in the dried basil and cook for 1 minute.
3. Add the diced tomatoes, chicken broth, and bring to a boil.
4. Add the tortellini and cook according to package instructions.
5. Stir in the chopped spinach and cook for another 2-3 minutes, until wilted.
6. Season with salt and pepper to taste. Serve warm, garnished with grated Parmesan.

Ham and Potato Soup

Ingredients:

- 2 cups diced ham
- 4 cups chicken broth
- 4 large potatoes, peeled and diced
- 1 onion, chopped
- 2 cloves garlic, minced
- 2 cups half-and-half or whole milk
- 2 tbsp butter
- 1 tsp thyme
- Salt and pepper to taste
- Chopped green onions for garnish

Instructions:

1. In a large pot, melt the butter over medium heat. Add the onion and garlic, cooking until softened, about 5 minutes.
2. Stir in the diced ham and cook for another 2 minutes.
3. Add the potatoes, chicken broth, thyme, salt, and pepper. Bring to a boil, then reduce heat and simmer for 20-25 minutes, or until the potatoes are tender.
4. Stir in the half-and-half and cook for another 5 minutes until the soup is heated through.
5. Serve warm, garnished with chopped green onions.

Avocado Soup

Ingredients:

- 2 ripe avocados, peeled and pitted
- 3 cups vegetable broth
- 1/2 cup Greek yogurt or sour cream
- 1/4 cup lime juice
- 1 small cucumber, peeled and diced
- 1 small onion, chopped
- 2 cloves garlic, minced
- 1 tbsp olive oil
- Salt and pepper to taste
- Fresh cilantro for garnish

Instructions:

1. Heat olive oil in a large pot over medium heat. Add the onion and garlic, cooking until softened, about 5 minutes.
2. Add the vegetable broth and bring to a simmer. Add the diced cucumber and cook for 5 minutes.
3. Remove from heat and let it cool for a few minutes.
4. In a blender, combine the avocado, cooked vegetable mixture, Greek yogurt, lime juice, salt, and pepper. Blend until smooth.
5. Chill the soup in the refrigerator for at least 30 minutes before serving.
6. Serve cold, garnished with fresh cilantro.

Sausage and Kale Soup

Ingredients:

- 1 lb Italian sausage (bulk or casings removed)
- 4 cups chicken broth
- 2 cups kale, chopped
- 2 large potatoes, peeled and diced
- 1 onion, chopped
- 2 cloves garlic, minced
- 1 tsp crushed red pepper flakes (optional)
- 1 cup heavy cream
- 1 tbsp olive oil
- Salt and pepper to taste

Instructions:

1. Heat olive oil in a large pot over medium heat. Add the sausage, breaking it up with a spoon as it cooks, until browned and cooked through.
2. Add the onion and garlic, cooking until softened, about 5 minutes.
3. Stir in the crushed red pepper flakes, chicken broth, and potatoes. Bring to a boil, then reduce heat and simmer for 15-20 minutes, or until the potatoes are tender.
4. Stir in the kale and cook for another 5 minutes.
5. Pour in the heavy cream and season with salt and pepper to taste. Heat through, then serve warm.

White Chicken Chili

Ingredients:

- 2 cups cooked, shredded chicken
- 4 cups chicken broth
- 2 cans (15 oz each) white beans, drained and rinsed
- 1 onion, chopped
- 2 cloves garlic, minced
- 1 can (4 oz) diced green chilies
- 1 tsp cumin
- 1/2 tsp oregano
- 1/2 tsp chili powder
- 1/2 tsp ground coriander
- 1 tbsp olive oil
- Salt and pepper to taste
- Fresh cilantro for garnish

Instructions:

1. Heat olive oil in a large pot over medium heat. Add the onion and garlic, cooking until softened, about 5 minutes.
2. Stir in the cumin, oregano, chili powder, and ground coriander, cooking for another 1-2 minutes.
3. Add the chicken, beans, chicken broth, and diced green chilies. Bring to a boil, then reduce heat and simmer for 20 minutes.
4. Season with salt and pepper to taste.
5. Serve warm, garnished with fresh cilantro.

Eggplant Soup

Ingredients:

- 2 large eggplants, peeled and cubed
- 1 onion, chopped
- 2 cloves garlic, minced
- 4 cups vegetable broth
- 1 can (14 oz) diced tomatoes
- 1 tsp dried basil
- 1 tsp ground cumin
- 1 tbsp olive oil
- Salt and pepper to taste
- Fresh parsley for garnish

Instructions:

1. Heat olive oil in a large pot over medium heat. Add the onion and garlic, cooking until softened, about 5 minutes.
2. Stir in the cumin and basil, cooking for another minute.
3. Add the eggplant, diced tomatoes, and vegetable broth. Bring to a boil, then reduce heat and simmer for 20-25 minutes, or until the eggplant is tender.
4. Use an immersion blender to blend the soup until smooth or blend in batches in a blender.
5. Season with salt and pepper to taste. Serve warm, garnished with fresh parsley.

Roasted Tomato and Basil Soup

Ingredients:

- 6 ripe tomatoes, halved
- 1 onion, chopped
- 3 cloves garlic, minced
- 4 cups vegetable broth
- 1/2 cup fresh basil, chopped
- 1 tbsp olive oil
- 1 tsp dried oregano
- Salt and pepper to taste
- 1/4 cup heavy cream (optional)

Instructions:

1. Preheat your oven to 400°F (200°C). Place the halved tomatoes on a baking sheet, drizzle with olive oil, and roast for 25-30 minutes, or until softened and slightly charred.
2. Heat olive oil in a large pot over medium heat. Add the onion and garlic, cooking until softened, about 5 minutes.
3. Add the roasted tomatoes, vegetable broth, oregano, salt, and pepper. Bring to a boil, then reduce heat and simmer for 15 minutes.
4. Use an immersion blender to blend the soup until smooth or blend in batches in a blender.
5. Stir in the fresh basil and heavy cream (if using). Heat through, then serve warm.

Sweet Potato and Carrot Soup

Ingredients:

- 2 large sweet potatoes, peeled and chopped
- 4 large carrots, peeled and chopped
- 4 cups vegetable broth
- 1 onion, chopped
- 2 cloves garlic, minced
- 1 tsp ground ginger
- 1/2 tsp ground cinnamon
- 1 tbsp olive oil
- Salt and pepper to taste
- Fresh parsley for garnish

Instructions:

1. Heat olive oil in a large pot over medium heat. Add the onion and garlic, cooking until softened, about 5 minutes.
2. Stir in the ginger and cinnamon, cooking for 1 minute.
3. Add the sweet potatoes, carrots, and vegetable broth. Bring to a boil, then reduce heat and simmer for 20-25 minutes, or until the vegetables are tender.
4. Use an immersion blender to blend the soup until smooth or blend in batches in a blender.
5. Season with salt and pepper to taste. Serve warm, garnished with fresh parsley.